DESERTS
OF THE
WORLD

by Natasha Branch

HOUGHTON MIFFLIN

BOSTON

TABLE OF CONTENTS

Introduction 4

Atacama Desert 6

Sahara Desert 8

Gobi Desert 10

Kalahari Desert. 12

Australian Desert 13

Mojave and Sonoran Deserts. 14

World Map: Deserts. 16

The Sahara is the world's largest desert.

INTRODUCTION

Deserts are land areas that get a lot of sunshine and little rain. Even when the rain comes, dry winds blow and evaporate the water. Few plants, animals, and people live in the desert because there is so little water. Without trees and plants, there is no shelter from the hot sun.

Most desert surfaces are covered in sand. Some are made up of rocks or stones. In some deserts, the rocks break up into small pieces because of the heat and quick, heavy rainstorms. The winds blow and move the levels of the ground surface. The sand or ground-up rocks form hills and valleys called dunes.

There are many kinds of deserts. Some deserts are hot all year long. Some deserts get cold in winter and at night, but get hot on summer days.

Nomads cross the desert with their camels.

There are many insects, reptiles, and small mammals living in the desert. Most are nocturnal, which means that they stay underground where it's coolest during the day and come out after the sun sets.

People do live in the desert. Some are nomads, wandering from one place to the next. Others settle in villages where there is water and vegetation.

Let's visit some of the deserts of the world.

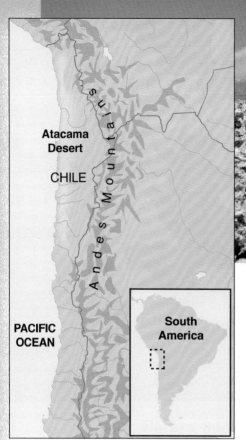

Large salt formations are found in the Atacama Desert.

ATACAMA DESERT

The Atacama Desert is in South America in the country of Chile. The Atacama is the driest desert in the world. It gets less than one half-inch of rain a year. Some parts have never had even one drop of rain!

The western part of the Atacama Desert runs along the Pacific Ocean. Fog that comes in from the ocean provides moisture, so there is some plant life.

The eastern part of the Atacama Desert is at the foot of the Andes Mountains. There is some rainfall there in the winter. Salt gathers at the mountain edges. The salt forms huge lumps that look like ice statues. Some of the Andes are volcanoes. The salt and volcanic ash in this area combine to make sodium nitrate. The Atacama is the only place in the world where you can find natural sodium nitrate. It is used for fertilizer and gunpowder.

For hundreds of years, miners came to the Atacama for sodium nitrate as well as copper, iron ore, lithium, and silver. Around World War I, sodium nitrate began to be made in a lab by people. Since then the miners have left, and the land has remained barren.

This may not be a bad thing. Because it is so dry in the Atacama, bacteria cannot live, so ancient objects are preserved. Archeologists have found 500-year-old relics there.

This ancient Incan relic was found in the Atacama.

SAHARA DESERT

The Sahara Desert is the world's largest desert. Located in northern Africa, the Sahara is 3 million square miles. That's about the size of the United States (without Alaska)! Much of the desert land is made up of sand seas. They are surrounded by big sand dunes molded by the high winds. Some dunes are 600 feet high!

The Sahara is very dry. Some areas don't see rain for many years. Only a small amount of rain comes for a very short time.

Some people herd sheep, goats, and cattle in the Sahara. Herders travel from one place to another by sleeping during the hot day and traveling at night.

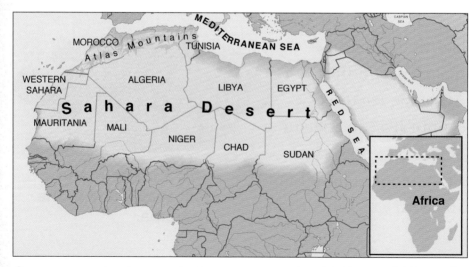

This town was built near an oasis in the Sahara.

In some areas of the desert, springs bring water from underground to the surface. Water helps plants grow. Plants include crops and shade trees. With food and shade, people can live. A desert village where people live is called an oasis. There are about 90 large oases in the Sahara. Each has fewer than 2,000 people living there. There are many small ones scattered throughout the Sahara. There isn't much water and plant life, so few people can live there.

Date palm trees at oases provide food and shelter from the heat. Crops such as barley and wheat are grown with the help of a human-made water system. Canals and pipelines bring water to the villages from far-off springs, wells, rivers, and streams.

GOBI DESERT

The Gobi Desert is the largest desert in Asia. It is hot in the summer, but it gets cold in winter. There is very little sand in this desert. Most of the surface is hard stone or gravel, called pavement.

The Gobi gets about 10 inches of rain a year, mostly in the summer. Very few plants grow in the Gobi. Animals have to travel far distances to find plant life for food. One plant that grows is a woody shrub called the saxaul (SAKS ahl). It has very few leaves and needs little water, so it can survive a drought, which is a period of days or months without water.

Gravel, not sand, covers much of the Gobi Desert.

Camels are animals that live well in the desert. They can go for many days without water. Their broad hooves do not sink in the sand. Their long eyelashes shield their eyes from the sand. Their humps are made of fat used by their bodies when there's no water or food.

A camel caravan is a long line of camels that go from one desert oasis to another. They carry all the food, supplies, and goods for trading, plus the travelers themselves. Camels can carry up to 600 pounds.

The camel in the Sahara is a one-humped Arabian camel called a dromedary. But in the Gobi and other Asian deserts there is a two-humped camel, the Bactrian. Though most are trained by humans to help with work, wild Bactrians still roam the desert.

Wild camels roam the Gobi.

Springboks, a type of quick antelope, live in Africa's Kalahari Desert.

KALAHARI DESERT

The Kalahari Desert, in southern Africa, features bright red sand dunes. It is not a typical desert. While most deserts have fewer than 10 inches of rainfall every year, some sections of the Kalahari get much more than that. Grasses grow there during the summer rainy season.

The Kalahari is home to many kinds of birds and reptiles. There are also antelope, lions, and hyenas. Kgalagadi Transfrontier Park is one of Africa's largest game reserves. Many tourists visit there for a rare glimpse of this wildlife.

AUSTRALIAN DESERT

Nearly one third of Australia is a desert. The Australian desert includes three deserts.

The Great Sandy Desert is the largest in Australia. It stretches along a long strip of beach on the Indian Ocean. Most of it is uninhabited – it has no oases and no people. Although this desert does get rain, mostly from thunderstorms, the water evaporates because it is so hot during the day. Because of this, there isn't much plant life.

The Great Victoria Desert features the lunette dune. It is hard and crescent shaped, like the moon.

Between these two deserts is the Gibson Desert. It is famous for its red sand hills called buckshot plains.

Aboriginal (AB uh RIJ uh nl) people still live in the Australian desert land. Aboriginal means "first to live in a country." The ancestors of the aboriginal people arrived from Asia more than 50,000 years ago.

MOJAVE AND SONORAN DESERTS

There are about 500,000 square miles of desert in North America. The Mojave (moe HAH vee) Desert is in southern California. It features Death Valley National Park. Pioneers named Death Valley after crossing the barren desert in 1849. Most of the Mojave is high but Death Valley is 282 feet below sea level, the lowest point in the United States. It is also very hot. Summer temperatures often reach 125°F.

South of the Mojave is the Sonoran Desert, which is mostly in Arizona. Colorful flowering plants grow there, with the help of winter rains. There are also a wide variety of cacti plants featuring prickly spines.

Cacti live on little water for a long time. Cacti have long roots to find water deep underground. The water is stored and protected from the sun in their thick, waxy stems.

There are about 2,000 types of cacti. They come in many shapes and sizes. One Sonoran cactus grows to be 40 feet tall!

Nevada

NORTH AMERICA

California

Mojave
Desert

Arizona

Sonoran
Desert

Mexico

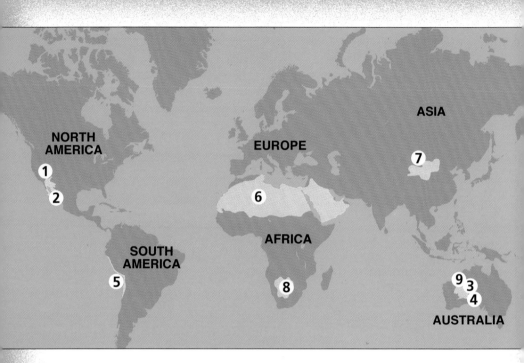

1. Mojave Desert
54,000 square miles
(140,000 square km)
high temperature
119°F (48°C)

2. Sonoran Desert
108,000 square miles
(275,000 square km)
high temperature
119°F (48°C)

3. Gibson Desert
60,250 square miles
(156,000 square km)
high temperature
108°F (42°C)

4. Great Victoria Desert
150,000 square miles
(338,500 square km)
high temperature
104°F (40°C)

5. Atacama Desert
40,600 square miles
(105,200 square km)
high temperature
95°F (35°C)

6. Sahara Desert
3.5 million square miles
(9 million square km)
high temperature
97°F (37°C)

7. Gobi Desert
500,000 square miles
(1.30 million square km)
high temperature
113°F (45°C)

8. Kalahari Desert
275,000 square miles
(712,250 square km)
high temperature
117°F (47°C)

9. Great Sandy Desert
130,000 square miles
(340,000 square km)
high temperature
108°F (42°C)